Eyes of Memory

Text by LENI SONNENFELD

Foreword by JAMES E. YOUNG

Eyes of Memory

Photographs from the Archives of HERBERT & LENI SONNENFELD

Yale University Press NEW HAVEN & LONDON

Designed by Richard Hendel.
Set in Minion type by Eric M. Brooks.
Printed in China by C&C Offset Printing.

Library of Congress Cataloging-in-Publication Data
Sonnenfeld, Leni
Eyes of memory: photographs from the archives
of Herbert and Leni Sonnenfeld / text by Leni
Sonnenfeld; foreword by James E. Young.
    p. cm.
ISBN 0-300-10605-x (alk. paper)
1. Sonnenfeld, Leni. 2. Sonnenfeld, Herbert,
1906–1972. 3. News photographers—United States—
Biography. 4. Jews—History—20th century—
Pictorial works. I. Title.
TR140.S637A3   2004
779'.990904924'0082—dc22   2004045820

A catalogue record for this book is available from the
British Library.

The paper in this book meets the guidelines for
permanence and durability of the Committee on
Production Guidelines for Book Longevity of the
Council on Library Resources.

10 9 8 7 6 5 4 3 2 1

Frontispiece: detail of p. 64.

Foreword JAMES E. YOUNG

"When does history become 'personal,'" the historian Susan Crane once asked, "when it is survived, or only when private lives become public knowledge?" For the German Jewish photojournalists Herbert and Leni Sonnenfeld, the answer was always both. At home in Berlin but forced out of his job when the Nazis came to power in 1933, Herbert began taking photographs of the life around him, chronicling the very events that turned him into a photographer. At first his wife, Leni, worked as his assistant, and then she too began taking pictures. Before long, their photographs of the Youth Aliyah, the flight of young German Jews to Palestine, were being printed in major magazines and newspapers around the world. Such photographs were both personal and historical: the extraordinarily powerful photographs Herbert took on his own exploratory trip to Palestine in 1933 brought Herbert and Leni numerous assignments to chronicle Jewish life in Berlin on the eve of its extirpation. Having been cursed to live in interesting times, the Sonnenfelds did not run for cover but instead opened their eyes wide to all that went on around them.

After emigrating to New York in 1939, they broadened their assignments to include the documentation of Jewish life as it replanted itself across Europe, Palestine, the Middle East, and North America. Herbert went to work as a photographer for Yeshiva University, where he focused primarily on Jewish events, historical figures, and personalities. Leni took a wider photographic view, traveling to Spain, Morocco, Yemen, Iran, Ireland, and Israel, among dozens of other lands, to cover day-to-day Jewish life in all its quotidian anonymity. Their photographs appeared in the *New York Times, Life,* the *Daily News,* the *Jewish Week, Esquire, Hadassah Magazine,* and dozens of reference works and exhibitions. By the time Herbert died in 1972, many of their photographs had become historical icons. Leni continued to take far-flung assignments, to publish and exhibit her photographs, and increasingly to manage single-handedly their combined archive of negatives. By the time Leni died in February 2004 at the age of ninety-six, what had begun as a personal quest to record the world around her had itself become a historic record.

v

The photographs are formally stunning and alive in their compositions and subjects. They are humanly proportioned, humane in their gentle, nonjudgmental focus. Despite the potential for fraught and darkly ominous images from this era, the photographs archived in this book remain full of the joy and excitement of life, a welcome counterpoint to the resolutely bleak picture we often have of Jewish life in these years. Portraits of thinkers like Martin Buber and artists like Max Lieberman accompany images of unknown Jewish athletes, students, and refugees. These images are, in the words of Sharon Mintz, curator of Jewish art at the library of the Jewish Theological Seminary, "at once iconic and intimate." The photograph of a young Jewish pioneer sowing seeds in a field, training for his emigration to Palestine, a frame filled mostly with sky and bisected by a razor-sharp horizon, captures the iconic idealism of Youth Aliyah and the determined expression of one young man—all of it animated by the blurred movement of seeds scattering in the wind. Like the other photographs in this collection, this one is preoccupied with life, not haunted by death.

This preoccupation with life is also evident in Leni Sonnenfeld's disarmingly plain-spoken essay, which in its conversational cadence captures the photographer's fundamental curiosity about, and embrace of, life. In a 1999 PBS film on the "poetry of aging" (*Grow Old with Me*), Sonnenfeld is shown examining dozens of images and long strips of negatives. "I have more than two hundred thousand negatives in my archive," she says as she views photograph after photograph of faces, all with their eyes seemingly focused on us. "They all have to do with people, with their histories, where they come from. But the most astonishing thing to my mind is that I almost never spoke the languages of these people. Eyes speak to each other, you know, without language. They have a language of their own." As we hold these images of faces in our hands now, we see what Sonnenfeld meant by the language of eyes, the memory implied from just behind them, the stories they tell without words.

When Leni Sonnenfeld titled this book *Eyes of Memory*, she was fully aware of its double meaning: it referred both to the eyes of her subjects (with their memory) and to her own photographic eye (with its memory). Indeed, according to the writer and journalist Sandee Brawarsky, a close friend of Leni's, none of these photographs could exist for the photographer without their own, sometimes highly personal stories. "Wherever you travel," Leni once told Sandee, "make sure you get invited into people's homes, so that you get to know who they are and how they live." That is, find the stories animating these people's lives and then tell them. In the photographs, some of these stories are evoked in the narrative movement between different parts of an image or between images, some of them are related by the photographer herself, and others seem to be implied by what may or may not be happening just beyond the borders of the frame.

Not long before Leni Sonnenfeld died, when it had become physically difficult for her to hold her heavy camera, she borrowed a friend's compact camera and continued taking pictures inside her apartment on Manhattan's Upper West Side. When even this became too hard for her, she suggested to Brawarsky that she could still happily "take pictures with her eyes." Sandee asked what that meant. Leni replied that it was just a matter of looking at and framing even the familiar world around her in new ways, seeing everything in the world as part of a composition, its own objet d'art. She always had an eye for embroidered textures and details but never allowed herself simply to gloss formal surfaces, preferring instead to go beneath and beyond to the implicit stories underlying such detail. "Wrinkles in photographs are delicious," Sonnenfeld once said. "They show that people have lived and suffered." In Sonnenfeld's eyes, then, wrinkles function as story-telling hieroglyphs, gesturing to lives, loves, and losses that are much more than just skin deep.

As a photojournalist, Leni Sonnenfeld sought to document and to illustrate the stories of others, both the writers and the subjects of news and magazine articles. But the photographs gathered in this collection might now be regarded as illustrations of her own story, the way she saw the world over the past sixty years. The result is a book of photographs quite unlike any other. In fact, as Leni Sonnenfeld suggests in her introductory essay, it may not be important to know what kind of book this is, whether it is photographic memoir or historical documentation, personal or public, history or memory. Like any archive, perhaps, it is all these things in varying degrees, image by image, year by year, page by page. Unlike other archives, however, there is nothing musty, old, or dead about this one. The photographs we hold in our hands from the Sonnenfeld archive pulse with life—as lived by their subjects and as recalled to us by the photographers.

Eyes of Memory   LENI SONNENFELD

This is not a memoir of my life. I start with a section of my life when everything was turned upside down because of Hitler; in a way it was a new beginning for me. So this "memoir" is just one small vignette of my life.

I had been married to Herbert Sonnenfeld for about two years when the Nazis came to power in 1933. When the Nazis actually became the legitimate government, we were all in shock. There was panic everywhere. But it was a silent panic, because it all took place within our own souls and chests. It was a time of confusion and disbelief, a time when people were so thrown out of their lives, out of the succession of days, of nights. We did not know what to think or do.

Herbert, like most Jews, lost his job overnight. All of us were left without means of support. As a young couple, we were especially at risk because there was no new employment available; we had absolutely no savings, because whatever Herbert earned at his job for a security alarm company was used up by us. We were faced with nothing, and there was no one to turn to, because the entire Jewish community was in shock.

Why we were so surprised is really a very strange thing to contemplate, because we knew that the Nazis were winning the election and that they were going to be in power. But when it actually happened, it came as a surrealistic experience. How is it possible, we wondered, that these barbarians are actually taking over everything?

My sister was married to one of the leaders of the Zionist organization. The Zionists were very well organized, because they had a definite goal. They were not like other German Jews who just wanted to be part of the German society. Zionists wanted to go to Palestine, to have their own country if possible, and to have a Jewish society; they saw that, again and again, Jews had been persecuted throughout the world and thrown out of every country they had ever lived in. They took great pride in being Jewish, in being part of that old, magnificent people. They were extremely effective organizers—they were all German, of course—but in fact they played a big role in establishing the confined community that now was isolated from the rest of German society.

Leni Sonnenfeld, Berlin, 1930s

There was a board that determined who could go to Palestine and who was not suited, for Zionist purposes, to be there. The British were in control of Palestine at that time, and they issued what were called certificates. There were certificates for so-called capitalists—that is, people with money—and there were certificates for workers, for young people who would build up the country. We went before the board thinking that this was our only way out of the dilemma we were in—to go to Palestine. But we were rejected because we were not strong, muscled workers; we were nice, middle-class young people who just needed a place to live.

After that rejection Herbert decided that he would try his luck by himself, that he would go to Palestine alone. At that time the Germans allowed Jews to leave the country and come back again, which means there was some semblance of freedom of movement. So he went, and he took along his little camera. Ever since he was a little boy, he had had a camera, and he loved photography. When I met him he was a great picture-taker.

After two or three weeks he returned to Berlin and said, "Never in a million years could I live in that country." Everything had been a shock to him. It was an underdeveloped, very poor country; it was hot, dusty, and disorganized. For instance, the buildings had no house numbers; he couldn't find any of the addresses he was given for contacts. He was disgusted with the whole thing.

But while he was there he took photographs, and when I saw them, I thought I'd never seen such magnificent pictures. I decided I had to show them to somebody, and the natural people to show them to were the Zionists, who had a large newspaper that sometimes carried illustrations, but primarily those were portraits of important people. It was at this time that photojournalism was just starting to develop.

I said to Herbert, "I've got to show them to Dr. Weltsch," who was the editor-in-chief of the Zionist newspaper. Dr. Weltsch looked at them, and without saying one word he pushed a button on his desk. In came all the employees, and he showed them the pictures. There was silence in the room. They were stunned, I think. They had never seen such pictures from Palestine. Dr. Weltsch asked me, "How much do you want for them?" and I thought "What? Money?" I didn't know that one could sell pictures; I had no idea. I just thought they were so wonderful that people ought to see them. He bought the pictures and published them, and the next day we received phone calls from all over Germany. There were many smaller magazines, small bulletins and newspapers; they all wanted Herbert's pictures, and

he got assignments to return to Palestine again and again. He became, overnight, a press photographer. As he grew busy, I became his assistant. Together we went on assignments and covered events.

Herbert had an innate knowledge of the process of photography. Though he never had a lesson, he never hesitated. I remember how touched I was when I saw him taking pictures, his hands trembling slightly at the excitement of the whole enterprise, and maybe betraying a bit of insecurity and anxiety about doing the right thing, pushing the right buttons, turning the right whatever-there-was on the machinery. I just watched him, and my heart really went out to him because he was so engaged in what he was doing, and every time it was a full success.

Herbert rigged up sort of a darkroom in our bathroom. He constructed a platform for the enlarger, and we got all the equipment together that was needed to wash the pictures, to fix them, and to dry them. We could work only at night because the bathroom was not a full-time darkroom—we would have needed black curtains, that sort of thing. We just worked together at night. He printed the pictures and I put them into the fixing chemical. And we had a great time, because everything that came up in the developing tray was a big success. There would be the image of what he had taken. It was really a very interesting and, in a way, successful time.

What Herbert recorded in his pictures were the negatives and positives of what was happening in the Jewish community, and how the lives of the Jews of Berlin had been organized into a working community with its own institutions, which of course existed before Hitler came to power—the welfare department for the poor, the religious organizations, and all the community businesses. But the important new part of it was that help had to be given to the helpless people who had to emigrate and wanted to emigrate, because outside the community, life was getting more ominous, more oppressive, day by day. There were always new ordinances, new rules telling Jews how to behave, what we were not allowed to do. Life became more and more dangerous. Frantic people were going to all the foreign consulates; they were sitting in the waiting rooms, hoping that other countries would relax their immigration rules and help by letting Jews come. But of course there were very few that did. There were never sufficient places. In the meantime, prisons filled up with Jews who had been arrested for no reason and who were maimed and beaten there.

Herbert's photography at the time showed mainly the life of the Jewish community, which, from the outside, looked quite normal. The sports clubs were functioning; the Jewish community had a sports field in the Grunewald, people went to sporting events, the young athletes trained. In 1933 came the advent of Youth Aliyah ("Ascent of the Youth"), a Palestine emigration program. Herbert documented the training of young people for life in Palestine, the schools that were opened for special workers in carpentry and mechanics—in any number of skills that young people could use to support their lives in Palestine—the language classes, the classes in biblical history and in the political history of Palestine. All these educational enterprises flourished.

The training and preparation culminated in the young people leaving their hometowns, their parents, their friends, their relatives. One of the most shattering experiences that Herbert and I witnessed, and were part of, was their leaving on trains, in large groups, with all their relatives and friends and parents and loved ones on the platform saying their goodbyes and waving the trains off. The heroism of those Jewish parents, to let their children go to that faraway, unknown, half-

Herbert Sonnenfeld, Berlin, 1930s

wild country with not only the possibility but, in many cases, the certainty that they would never see them again, is beyond description. I think that this sacrifice to preserve the next generation of Jewish existence is not only heroic but one of the most moving deeds, the most moving experiences. I looked at these people and my heart broke in two. Young as I was, I could feel the dreadful, dreadful tearing apart of their emotions. I could feel how bereft they were at letting go of their precious children.

While that Youth Aliyah endeavor went on, of course with the great support of the Zionist organization, the Jüdischer Kulturbund (Jewish Cultural Society) was created by the Jewish community. The Kulturbund put on astounding productions of operas, operettas, and plays, and it sponsored poetry readings and concerts with famous soloists. The events were frequented by the Jewish community, but Nazis attended as well, not only to watch over the proceedings to see that nothing forbidden was happening, but also to enjoy them, because all the performers had been professional actors, dancers, and musicians who were part of German institutions long before Hitler. Many of them were the most charming and accomplished of performers.

During that time all the welfare institutions were functioning full force. People had to be provided with clothing, with food; in the wintertime they had to be housed in places with enough heat. It was a supreme effort not only to have our people survive, but also to give them hope, any kind of hope! We all lived with the illusion that one day everything would change, and many probably wished for things to go back to the way they were before Hitler, in spite of the obvious consent of the German people. But deep down we knew that this was never to be.

Herbert and I did not experience the dreadful happenings when people were deported, many to Poland. Children were taken from their parents in Germany and deported to Warsaw, to the ghetto. One of my nephews was among them, and he lived and perished in the ghetto with all the others. While we were still in Berlin, we saw the parks segregated—there were benches marked "for Jews only." We were also subjected to an 8 p.m. curfew, which meant that Jews could not go to see a movie or go to the theater or be out in the street. All we could do was stay home and listen to the radio, which we did. We were not allowed to listen to any foreign radio programming, but we defeated that. I remember sitting with blankets over our heads and over the radio, listening to the BBC.

One day toward the end of 1936, the bell of our apartment rang, and two burly men introduced themselves as coming from the Gestapo. They asked to come in, and of course we had to invite them. It turned out that they wanted to interrogate us about certain ideas or reports they had in their files. So we all sat down and they pulled out two writing pads and started with their questions. They accused Herbert of having been seen taking pictures of strategic points in the city—of bridges, of river crossings, of railway stations. Why and for whom was he doing this? Herbert said, "I have done no such thing. I have no intention and no idea about taking such pictures, because according to the laws, I am permitted only pictures within the Jewish community. This report is a false one." They wrote that down, and they asked all sorts of questions about our livelihood and about our relations with people in the building.

They asked for our passports, which we still had. They were the regular passports; I believe that we had added our new middle names, Sarah for women and Israel for men—we wouldn't have dared not to. When I handed over my passport, they saw that I had been to Sweden and England. They asked me about the purpose of my trips, so I told them that I had gone to take pictures of a Swedish training facility for Jewish boys and girls who were preparing to immigrate to Palestine. There they were trained in agriculture and learned Hebrew—the usual preparation for life in Palestine. In England I had visited a cousin who had immigrated to Manchester. I had also taken some pictures of Jewish sites and people, and that was all. They took note of everything on their big pads, and they must have asked about many other things, because their visit lasted at least an hour.

Finally they became, in a way, friendlier. Maybe they liked us; I don't know what it was. In the end they tore the papers from their pads and ripped them up, saying, "Well, everything seems to be all right with you," and they thanked us for our time, and we walked them to the door. Once outside, they turned around, raised their arms, and said, "Heil Hitler." It was their farewell to us. We silently closed the door and threw ourselves on the couch in our one-room apartment and breathed a deep sigh of relief. But we realized that the time had come to leave this place, that this was just a small warning of what was to come.

In September 1939, when the Nazis marched into Poland, we were absolutely desperate, sure that it was too late for us, that we were caught in Germany. The news had come over the radio, "Achtung! Achtung! Our troops just entered Poland"—they didn't use the word "invaded," but everybody knew what they meant.

The next day we received a telegram from the American consulate to come immediately to get our visas, because they, of all people, realized that this step by the Germans meant war. This was the last chance for America to save the handful of Jews who were registered with the consulate, who had their affidavits, who had their papers ready, and who had been on the waiting list for two years and more. We ran to the consulate and got the visas, and two months later we were on our way to Trieste, from where we sailed to New York.

But there were a lot of things to do before that. Right after we got the visas we were ready to start packing. We were allowed to take only one big suitcase for the two of us, and we had to decide what to take and what to leave, which was most of our possessions. The German authorities required us to list everything we were taking with us. So we started making lists the minute we had our things sorted, and we were extremely careful to list every little thing we packed—pins, even—so as not to jeopardize our departure.

When Herbert and I started sorting our belongings, which were not very many, he also went through his negatives. I shudder to remember that he actually threw out negatives, irreplaceable negatives! Whatever was on them was precious in history. But he took only the ones that he liked, that he thought were good images, and the ones that were directly relevant to the destruction of the German Jewish community. Somehow we got our enlarger into that suitcase, along with the negatives and prints we had, and our personal belongings. We left everything else behind in the apartment, just the way it was. The hardest decision was to leave behind my little dog. She was my substitute child, a lovely, spirited wire-haired terrier, who was a real wild one, a naughty one, a sweet one. But there was no choice. We had to leave her in Berlin, and my sister took her. And after we got to New York, my sister wrote to me that she refused to eat. She would lie in her corner, just sleeping a lot, and she was in mourning, I think, and longing for us just as we were for her.

In the end, no inspector came to inspect the lists or the contents of the suitcase, and we took the train from Berlin to Trieste. We traveled through the country to the south. Everything was blacked out; there was no light anywhere, even at the railway stations. But when we arrived at the Italian border, suddenly all the lights went on. The Italian border was lit up, and it was like a symbol of freedom that we came from that darkness into the light.

The voyage to the United States took, I think, more than two weeks. Upon our arrival at one of the many piers on the West Side of Manhattan, we were herded into one of the large rooms on the ship. Customs officials had boarded the ship to do preliminary work on our papers. We were kept in line by ropes on either side of us, and slowly we pushed on. Once the papers were reviewed and everything was determined to be in order, we were slowly herded out by the same procedure, the two ropes on each side. At the bottom of the gangplank there was an American policeman, and when we passed him, he said in a very low, private voice, "Shalom." We didn't know that he was Jewish, but when he said shalom to us . . . I still get a knot in my throat when I think of it. We were so shaken up by that one word, "Peace," that even now my tears are almost ready to fall. We never in our lives knew of a Jew to be a policeman. This was our welcome to America, and it was really very emotional and exciting.

Herbert's brother and his wife were waiting for us; the American Jewish Congress had prepared two brownstone houses on the Upper West Side for the refugees. One house was for women and one for men, and they even separated the husbands from their wives. We stayed in the brownstone houses for about three weeks, until we had rested and gotten a feel for the city. When the Congress was ready to let us go, they provided a furnished apartment.

After a few weeks we started to look for our own apartment. The change in housing in New York has been so tremendous that it almost sounds like a fairy tale when I say that we had a choice of apartments that was incredible. We wanted to live on the West Side, preferably along Central Park West because we loved the park and it was a lovely section of the city. So we walked along Central Park West, and there was not one building that did not have vacancies. There had been overbuilding; landlords were quite desperate at the time and were offering concessions of two, three, or even four months' rent. That was of course very seductive, but still, we had no money, or very, very little of it. So we took an apartment that was within our means, the means being support from some Jewish organization, because we hadn't earned any money yet. It was a ground-floor apartment on Central Park West, quite dark and dismal.

One day when I came home—I had gone to explore the city and perhaps visit a possible client, or possibly I went shopping—Herbert opened the apartment door for me, and he had an unusual expression on his face. I said, "What is it? Has something happened?" He said, "No . . . " And I walked into the living room, and there in the middle of the room sat a little white fluffy ball, which jumped up when

I entered. Herbert had gotten me a little white wire-haired terrier, a puppy to substitute for my little dog whom I had to leave in Berlin. I was in tears and delighted with that little thing; it was so adorable and such a comfort to me.

Around the same time we made our first sale from the pictures that we had brought along—I think they were from the Palestine series. We sold it to the Jewish National Fund for $75. Now $75 represented a small fortune to us, and we were very happy with it. We proudly deposited the check in our first savings account. I still have our first three or four savings account bank books, which show deposits of $6, of $8, and a withdrawal of $4, which we quickly replaced with new savings of maybe $5. It shows how bent we were on saving money and on living frugally.

The American Jewish Congress rented for us what was then considered a studio. It was a one-room apartment on Union Square in which Herbert had a darkroom and could resume his career as a photographer. So we started to work in earnest, thanks to the Jewish National Fund and its publication of the photographs. Many Jewish organizations were very interested in Herbert's work, and they gave him assignments. So he started working, and slowly, slowly, he worked for practically every Jewish organization in the city. He was kept very busy, and we earned a pretty decent living from the start, which was quite amazing.

Herbert attended a very important meeting—the so-called Biltmore Conference, which happened in May 1942. The conference was named after the Biltmore Hotel in midtown Manhattan, where it was held. All the leading lights in Jewish life were present—Chaim Weizmann (who was then just a scientist, an ardent Zionist), David Ben-Gurion, Nahum Goldmann, Rabbi Stephen Wise, and many other well-known American Zionists—and they are all in the picture of them sitting on the dais. It was a remarkable meeting of all these people. They discussed everything concerning Jewish life in the communities of the whole world. Herbert was the only photographer present, and his pictures are highly important documents of Jewish life at that time.

Later in 1942 Herbert was drafted into the army. He was not a citizen yet, but at the time soldiers were needed, so aliens were drafted into the army and made citizens during basic training. He was sent to a training camp in Virginia, I believe. He was by that time already thirty-six years old, the oldest of the recruits, but he went through basic training with flying colors. He went on long, arduous marches and was determined to keep up with all the eighteen- to twenty-one-year-old soldiers.

And he did it. Shortly after he finished his basic training he was sent to England. He went to Litchfield barracks, a large reception camp for American soldiers who were sent to Europe. The commander of this camp liked Herbert so much that he made him the camp photographer because he wanted to keep him in the camp.

After the war ended Herbert was sent to headquarters in Frankfurt, Germany, and given a special task. He was to read Hitler's private mail, which consisted of letters that the German people had sent to their "beloved Führer." There were many American soldiers who were fluent in German, but he was one of the few who could read the so-called Gothic script, which was used by the German population of a certain age. So he was supposed to go through the mail and decide which letters were worth keeping and which ones should go into the wastebasket because they were of no interest. It is hard to imagine this today, when every shred of the past, of history, is so precious that it is almost holy. And it is incredible to think that letters directed to the most notorious man in Europe were left to a soldier to read and make momentous decisions about. But this is what he did. And he sent me two letters to show what the German people had to communicate to their beloved Führer. I was absolutely amazed by the fervor, the sexuality, the adoration that was in these letters. They addressed him as "my much-beloved Führer." They wrote of their dreams about him. They wrote about their unhappy marriages. They confided in him. They adored him. It was an outpouring of trust and love.

As for me, I had taken up photography even before leaving Germany and had gone to Sweden in 1936 to take pictures. When Herbert left for the army I picked up where he left off. We still got assignments, which I tried to fulfill, and I got more and more proficient at it.

One of my really big assignments was of Camp Fort Ontario, near Oswego, in upstate New York. It was in 1943 or 1944. It was a project that President Roosevelt had sponsored; it consisted of an emissary, the writer Ruth Gruber, going to Europe and collecting refugees—Germans and people of other nationalities, some Jews, some not—who were in Italian concentration camps. The refugees had been selected before Ruth Gruber got there, but she was to gather them onto one of the Liberty Ships and bring them to America. There were close to a thousand refugees—families with children, actors, musicians. I don't know who made these selections, but it looks as if the choices were made by a group eager to save children and talented and capable people. This is a horrible thing in a way, because to tell people in the camps, "You can go but not you. Not you, but you can," seems very cruel and must have been extremely hard to do.

The more I worked, the more experience I gathered, and I had the pleasure of being given a totally free hand by many of those who gave me the assignments. I did a lot for Jewish organizations that were conducting fundraising operations for their projects. I believe that they trusted me to get the sort of images that they needed and wanted. It was different when I had assignments from the *New York Times* or other newspapers. Then of course I went by whatever they planned to run in their publications. But the organizations left it entirely to me, and that gave me a wonderful sense of freedom. Whatever satisfied me, I was sure, would satisfy them, because I knew exactly what they needed. I was careful to pick—not all the time, but often—very appealing children or young people, so whatever was used in the publications would appeal to their readership. To that extent I was quite conscious of the choices that I made, because there is no way around it: people do respond to the beauty of the human face, to expression, to charm. I had a great sense of the importance that eyes play in the human face, as they do in animal faces. The eyes really are the mirror of the soul.

I have always wondered about and marveled at the infinite variety of expression, of communication, of so many different aspects of our feelings and thoughts that go into the eyes or come from the eyes toward us. How is it possible that these two little round balls can express anger, hatred, rejection, sadness, happiness, joy, disdain—any possible human emotion? How is it possible that all this can be expressed through the eyes of a human? Of course I know that it all comes from the commander in chief, the brain—from the brain directly into the eyes and out into the world. But how is it that even babies respond to the language of the eyes?

The eye contact that comes from an image and meets the eye of the viewer is very powerful. Some feel that such an image is too posed. I, to the contrary, feel that the averted glance of a person in an image is the posed one. Eye contact has a magnetic feel to it, and I am often drawn back to the images of photographers who speak to me so directly. I want to have that meeting of the eyes again. When I processed pictures in the darkroom, when the eyes came out in the developer, slowly, slowly taking their complete form, it was a fascinating thing to behold, because out of nothing, out of the developer chemicals, came that talking eye.

My work engrossed me totally. I never considered it a business, although it was of course our means of support, our livelihood—but it always came to me as a fresh experience, and it was such a pleasure.

Not that I had all these considerations while I was taking the photographs. That came to me without any forethought or preparation. I may have said "look at me" or "listen" and people responded, turning their eyes to me and to the camera. But this wish of mine was quite natural for me. I didn't think: I want to have this picture this way or that way. It was much more intuitive and of that particular small moment. On the other hand, when I think of all the drama of the "ingathering of the exiles," when all these emotions and passions poured out of the people into the camera without any participation on my part, I photographed what was happening before my eyes—the embraces, the tears, the helplessness and the tiredness, and the excitement of these people returning home. There the camera really took over, and there was no point in adding to that dramatic and very compelling moment.

This moment is very strong in me: the chapter about the ingathering of the exiles; that is, the period in the early 1950s when an infant among nations, inexperienced and endangered—the new nation of Israel—took in hundreds of thousands

Leni Sonnenfeld, Israel, 1965

of immigrants. The whole country opened its arms wide and turned itself into a sort of Noah's Ark, not just taking in two of each species but taking in the lame, the unfit physically and mentally, the old and the young. As Moses said when Pharaoh offered to free only the men of Egypt from slavery, "We will go with our young and with our old, with our sons and with our daughters, with our flocks and with our herds" (Exodus 10:9).

Israel took in this flood of immigrants from a hundred different nationalities; the people of Israel readily took on the new tax burdens and all the hardship and all the upheaval that such a number of immigrants would cause to a tiny place like Israel. It was one of the most inspiring events that one can imagine. And strange as it may seem, I often think that without the Hitler scourge, we would have never felt this strong emotional commitment, this powerful sense of the Jewish people, of what we really are, and of what great contributions to culture and the civilization of humanity we have made. The people of Israel with one voice embraced all these strangers who spoke so many different languages, who did not know Hebrew except the Hebrew of the Bible, who were the outcasts of so many countries, and who wanted to live in their own country. As Emma Lazarus said, they were "yearning to breathe free."

I was asked more than once, "How is it that you have photographed so many poor people, that you never took pictures of the famous, of the rich, even of the middle class? How come?" And to that I can only answer that the twentieth century was what I call the "century of the refugees." Were there ever, in the history of humanity, more people who were, as they so nicely call it, "displaced"? More people uprooted from their homes, their countries? Were there ever so many people homeless? So I chose the "have-nots" because that was (and still is) where my heart goes.

Anti-Semitism has made the Jews the eternal refugee and has created what is laughingly called "the wandering Jew," as if it were the desire of the Jewish people to wander, to have new "adventures." Why, nothing could be further from the minds of the Jewish people, who wanted only to bring up their families, to raise them to be good citizens, to respect the laws, to be part of the communities they lived in, to be accepted. That was the yearning for over two thousand years of the wandering Jews. That was the reason for the flood of refugees coming to Israel to make a place where they would be accepted without question, without reservation, where they were offered a place of their own to live, to work, to love. People in these tattered ships would walk down the gangplank supporting their old, holding them up, often with the babies in their mothers' arms or clinging to their fathers; people would throw themselves on the ground and kiss the earth. When they came down that gangplank, having been seasick, I could see in their haggard faces life and hope awakening in them. It was overwhelming. It was overwhelming.

The huddled masses of Ellis Island came to America to find a better livelihood. For Jews coming to Israel it was much more than that. They were coming home, where they would be received with love, where there would be peace, where there would be a place for their children to grow up without being the recipients of hatred, without having to hate back. It was paradise for them.

I remember the port of Haifa being decorated with huge signs, greeting the ships and the people in them with "Welcome" in I don't know how many different languages. There was always a festive air over the harbor. There were always people waiting behind the fences, hoping to greet their relatives, their friends, who were on that ship, coming home. There was an excitement, there were so many tears, there were so many embraces, it was a great "affair," a celebration.

I want to say one more thing about the ingathering of the exiles. This particular experience was one of the strongest and most beautiful, and at the same time most dreadful, of my life. What I as an individual felt was an amazing closeness to all those very strange people whom I never would have recognized as being Jews. It wasn't a religious closeness, but I felt that we Jews were archetypal people. They seemed biblical to me. They seemed larger than life and much smaller than life, and oppressed, and full of despair, and hope, and expectancy, because most of them, if not all, had been leading the lives of slaves or of people who had never been accepted as members of the countries they came from. Many came from North Africa speaking Arabic. It is not possible to describe fully the masses, the size of the families, with so many infants, so many toddlers. It was an incredible, incredible experience. And I, who was in the wonderful position of keeping it all alive in photography, was privileged to have witnessed it and to have been able to fix it for others to see. I was lucky most of all to be in the place where it actually happened.

I undertook many travels to fulfill assignments, and the schools and educational places that I visited everywhere I went were an entirely different and very uplifting experience. The main purpose of my presence in Morocco in 1970 was an assignment that I received from ORT, a wonderful organization that was founded in Russia in 1880 (its name is an abbreviation for a Russian term meaning the Society for Trades and Agricultural Labor). Its schools and training centers are now located all over the world, and they have an excellent reputation for preparing their Jewish and non-Jewish students for the realities of life. The organization used my photographs as a record of their activities for many years, and I had the good fortune to be assigned to many countries. On all these trips I met a great many people and was invited to holidays, weddings, and bar mitzvahs, and these events gave me wonderful insights into the life of those communities.

One bar mitzvah ceremony in Casablanca not only taught me but also let me experience a revelation. Of course I had been to many bar mitzvahs in my life, and I was rather bored with them, but in Casablanca this turning point in a boy's life—what it really meant—was revealed to me. I had known that it occurred at the age of thirteen when a boy supposedly becomes a man, but I had never really understood the importance of that celebration, because I had never before been in contact with a Sephardic community.

After the boy had made his address to the assembled congregation, it was time to celebrate his becoming a man and a member of the community. This is the first time a Jewish boy puts on tefillin, the phylacteries that Jewish men use during morning prayers, consisting of two small black boxes with black straps attached. One box is placed on the arm with the straps wrapped around seven times, and the other box sits on the forehead. And inside the boxes are biblical verses. This boy stood in front of the place where the Torahs are kept in a shrine, and one by one people came up to him. It started with his grandparents—the grandfather, the grandmother. Each of them wound that leather band around the boy's arm one turn, and embraced and kissed him. And one by one his father came, his mother came, his brothers and sisters, his uncles, his aunts, his cousins, his friends, one by one they came, and each wound the tefillin one turn around the arm, and they embraced and kissed him.

It had such power, this outpouring of love, this adherence to the age-old customs. It came upon me as a revelation because he was so visibly and audibly taken into this community. It was extremely moving, and very educational to me.

An assignment from a new magazine took me to Iran in 1973. I admired the beauty and regal posture of the tall women wrapped in the long chador, a discreetly flowered big shawl covering them from head to toe. Subtle differences in this way of dressing had ritual meaning, I was told; some women were strictly orthodox,

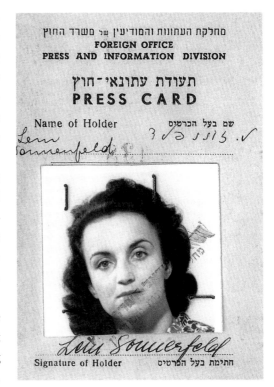

Leni Sonnenfeld's Israeli press pass

some less so, and others wore the garment merely as a traditional custom, followed even by very young women. Whenever those women jumped onto the curb from the street—which one had to do because there was always water running along the curb—the garment opened a little, and under that garment they were dressed in miniskirts, which was the fashion then, and clearly an expression of the wish to be modern and part of Western culture.

Life in Iran at that time, under the Shah, seemed quite Western. The high-rise buildings in Tehran could have been anywhere in the world. The streets were modern and had a familiar look about them. Not so the old bazaars, which were seductive and interesting; they were filled with men who worked at their great craft of embossing huge metal plates and all kinds of ornaments and wall hangings. They were very skilled, and these markets were just clanging away with the noises of the tools they used. It was very, very different from any other place that I had known before that time. And it fascinated me. All the street advertising was up to date— for all the big corporations of that time, from IBM to all the latest car makers and gasoline producers and Coca-Cola—and dominated the city; it must have been a great irritant to the clergy who resented the Westernization of Iran.

I went to the university and met a number of students who were at that time very much attracted to democracy and displayed great curiosity about the West. One had the feeling that the country was yearning to modernize and to be part of the world. Very near Tehran there was a place called Rey, where people sent their Persian rugs to be washed. It was at a lake where one could see women washing their clothes. The rugs were spread out on the shore, and men washed the rugs with big brooms or scrubbers. And what did they use? Tide, the American-made detergent. After the washing, the rugs were spread out to dry on the rocks that surrounded that lake, and it was quite a sight.

From the time of ancient, highly cultured Persia, the populace revered their poets and artists. While walking in the center of Tehran, I discovered large meeting places whose open interiors attracted a great many people. Not knowing Farsi, I did not comprehend what was going on. Much to my surprise and admiration, I learned that these were readings of poetry.

I also visited many of the workplaces where they printed beautiful old Persian designs on cloths for bedcovers, for tablecloths, for wall hangings. It was arduous work. They used the most primitive means for the printing. Wood blocks with the design were tied to their hands, which were covered with thick bandages; to print the design onto the cloth they dipped the block in some kind of dye. Then they hit that hand sharply with the other hand, and that put the design on the cloth. So their hands must have been swollen day and night and very painful in spite of all the bandaging and the upholstery that they put between the two hands.

When I left Iran in October 1973, I had been booked to fly from Tehran to Tel Aviv. I asked the steward on board the plane, "When will we land in Tel Aviv?" He looked at me in amazement and said, "We don't go to Tel Aviv." I asked, "Why not?" And he said, "Don't you read the papers? Don't you listen to the radio? There's a war on in Israel." It was the time of the Yom Kippur War. And I in my innocence said, "But I've got to go to Tel Aviv! What am I to do?" And he said, "I'm afraid you can't go to Tel Aviv because we are going straight to London, and you've got to go with us."

Once I arrived in London, I thought, "Well, the war can't take too long, perhaps three days." At that time we thought the Israeli army was invincible, and I was thinking of the Six-Day War. But of course this war was not finished in three days. After I had waited for about a week in London, I still thought that it couldn't be long before all would calm down.

One morning I took a walk and passed a travel agency with very beautiful photographs of Spain in the window. I had never been there before—we had boycotted Franco's Spain because of his alliance with Germany and that brutal civil war. None of my friends, none of my acquaintances, ever touched Spanish soil for many years after. But I did not want to sit in London waiting for the war to end, so I got myself a ticket to Madrid, and before I knew it I landed in Spain.

I had no assignments. I came totally unprepared; I did not know what to expect. But I soon found that there were actually very few Jews in Spain at this time. There were schools and small shops, but the Jewish presence was minimal. I traveled around in buses, because that is one of the wonderful ways to see any place. I was a tourist. I looked for the famous sights, as the guidebook said. I looked for historical places. And every step one takes in Spain rewards one with its beauty and its fullness of life. I found the people very different from those in northern European countries. They were very serious people. You hardly saw a smile. What they had survived was not easily dismissed from their minds and their hearts. So many people had lost their lives, had lost their families, fighting their own people in that dreadful civil war. On that visit there was barely any tourism because the country was not ready for it, but on later visits to Spain, I saw remarkable recovery.

Around 1978 a new Jewish magazine appeared on the scene, and in one of the initial issues it published my series on the Jewish community in Iran. The editors wanted more material, and when I suggested a story on the Jewish community in Gibraltar, they enthusiastically gave me an assignment.

Gibraltar is very beautiful, situated as it is at the gateway of the Mediterranean between the southern tip of Spain (it is a peninsula of Spain, actually) and North Africa. It had been a fortress and a colony of the British Empire for more than two hundred years. Many North African Jews settled there—they came from Morocco, from Tunisia, from Algiers—and formed a prosperous and interesting community. The chief minister of Gibraltar at the time, Sir Joshua Hassan, was a Jew, and so was the minister of commerce and development. Many of the streets were named after these and other prominent Jews, and it was astonishing to see the importance and influence of that community.

There were several synagogues, all very beautiful, small places with interesting architecture. The old Jews' Cemetery contained unusual gravesites. There was one, for instance, of five famed rabbis. The gravestones had a little gate around them, and they were like a family, buried there side by side. They also have a custom I never had heard of before: the sons burying their parents. They carry the bodies in their arms and descend into the graves to place the bodies directly into the earth, and after that is done, they cover the grave with a slab of stone and sand. This practice shows a loving, accepting sensibility vis-à-vis the Western customs of burial and speaks of closeness that no formal burial in a fancy coffin can express.

The old-age homes were quite luxurious. Each person had his or her own room, or more than one room, with a view toward the Mediterranean. The residents were very well taken care of and lived in great dignity. There were no very poor Jews there, and the community saw to it that their old were cared for until they died.

At this point I would like to talk a bit about my photography—that is, the selection I have made to go into this book. I have after all these years made a discovery about it; it was something that I never thought of before, because there was no reason to examine my actions. But now I have come to realize that my intense dislike of speed, of fast action, in life has transferred itself, totally subconsciously I am sure, onto my work. I like the contemplative vision of life, of living. And so I see now that my images are first of all of individuals at rest, at peace with themselves, however temporarily, because they were having their photograph taken. But

I prefer the meeting of eyes, which is a stopping point. It is not action. Both photographer and subject are at rest, taking their time and really looking at each other. I have the feeling, when I walk in the street, that nobody really looks at anybody else. Of course they are looking, but not in the way I just described. It is so fleeting and so superficial, but when I look at the images, there is some sort of expectation in the eyes of the subjects—I hate to call them subjects, because they are very real people to me—expectation, but also a quiet really seeing.

This wish to escape from action, from the pace of today's life—I know now why I was motivated to go into old-age homes and look at the lives of all those widows, who lost husbands and probably children, and whom other children may have just deposited there. These old, lonely women moved me, sometimes to tears. They were quiet and resigned or depressed. It weighed on me very powerfully, that this was the end of these women's lives, which were probably all along filled with the care of others or whatever destinies they had. It all ended here.

It is interesting to see how very different Herbert's pictures are from mine. It is of course to be expected that two people would see things from their own points of view, from their own sensibilities. But his were much more spontaneous; he responded very much to the comic aspects of human activity. He had the eye of a painter, which he, after retirement, became in earnest. A few years before he died in 1972, he gave up photography in order to paint. He turned out to be a very gifted painter, and his life was immeasurably enhanced and blessed toward the end by his love for painting.

His way of looking at life and looking at people's behavior had to be different from mine because his childhood, his whole life, had been so different from mine. I used to lean toward the darker side because of my childhood experiences. I lost my mother through illness when I was eight years old. I was a middle child: I had two older sisters and a younger brother and sister. I was the child who was not paid much attention to, because the older ones were already out on their own. They were fifteen and sixteen when my mother died, and the younger ones were five and seven, and they were the babies of the family who got special attention. So I was on my own, which I continue to be. And life looks different to people who have a different standing in the family and who carry the wounds of their childhood with them all their lives. Other influences come later on, but the basic conditions are laid very early and play a very big part in any person's life.

Quite contrary to the common belief that photographers are observant people—they see everything and master everything—I found that I am quite unobservant, that I really see only the thing that interests me one way or the other. As a rule I was focused on what I wanted to do at the moment, and everything else would only have distracted me and taken away my concentration.

I remember that editors who had commissioned me to do a story asked, upon my return, to see the contacts. When I brought them the contacts, they said, "What is this? You took just one shot of this and one shot of that? Don't you have contact sheets the way we get them from other photographers?" And I realized that they were used to looking at thirty-six images of the same head shot of some important personality or not-so-important personality, and I could never get over my astonishment when I saw these thirty-six exposures of one head looking a bit to the left, a little more to the left, a little more to the left, looking up, looking down, looking to the right side again and again. There was so little difference between the images that I thought, "It is not possible to take that many pictures of the same person and not have him or her change the way he sat, the way he stood." I quite often, perhaps most of the time, took one or two shots of a person. I was convinced that I did not want more because I had what I felt was the picture. So that was one aspect of being a different photographer—being perhaps a bit more daring than other photographers because I had the arrogance to be sure that this was the right picture, and I had no desire to take more pictures of that same person.

Years back, of course, color photography was rare. The purists among photographers to this day say, "I prefer black and white." I love black and white pictures, and I love color pictures. I love the vibrancy of these ravishing colors. I find that black and white is more dramatic and that a color picture is, perhaps, too pretty, but they are two different media to me. I don't think one can compare the two. First of all, it depends on what is in the picture. I think that a black and white landscape loses a lot because a wider vista is infinitely more interesting in all the shadings, the subtlety of colors. Not so a portrait perhaps. But I love them both. Of course color photography is now practically the rule for all publications because printing in color has become much cheaper and easier to do.

There is one thing that I have to add to all I have said. Whenever I went back to a place that had left its mark on my heart, to see it again, the shock was so dreadful—as in the case of that ancient cemetery in Prague, which is famous all over the world. That cemetery has never failed to leave a lasting and very deep impression on people of all kinds, but I think especially on a photographer like me. When I went there for the first time in 1966, it was overwhelming in its desolation, in its expression of a whole community.

The Jews, eight hundred years ago, were given a very small area to bury their dead, less than two city blocks. That small place must have filled up very soon, because people die every day. And they did not know what to do. So they started burying their dead on top of each other, meaning that from the first graves they were aware that no more space could be had from the city to serve as their cemetery, and they must have buried their dead much deeper than was customary. They had to make more room for the dead all through these hundreds of years, so they buried them on top of previous layers of dead and their tombstones. There were many layers of tombstones peeking out from the earth in various sizes, not in any kind of arrangement, they were just all over, and the earth and the paths were very narrow and much trodden, and the trees were large. It was a place of such indelible impression that anyone who has visited it could never forget it.

When I returned in 1991 on my second or third trip to Prague, I hardly recognized the place. In that short time it had undergone such change that I could not understand what had happened. They had cut down trees; they had widened the

Leni Sonnenfeld, New York, 1957

Leni Sonnenfeld, New York, 1995.
Photograph © Vera Isler.

21

pathways where people could walk. The small tops of the tombstones that came up from under the earth had all disappeared. The place was very orderly and clean, it seemed to me, and in some corners it did not even resemble the cemetery, because there were tombstones without inscriptions, there were tombstones cut up like pieces of sculpture, without any identification. There was an older part that still had big tombstones, but the general impact of that place was totally gone, and this put me into a turmoil of incomprehension and rage. I was outraged that anybody had dared to touch that almost holy place. It seemed sacrilegious, it seemed a destruction, it seemed unacceptable. It all was done to accommodate the tourists who were drawn to this famous place, to experience that particular square of earth.

What I want to say at this moment is that going back to a cherished place is so hazardous and can be so disillusioning and sad that I would advise never going back to a place that one loved and that was so revealing in its history, in its importance, in its respect for the dead, in its respect for the lives they have led.

Yet when I look back at my life as a photographer, I see the satisfaction and the joy and the comfort that photography has been in my life. I believe that photography was not considered an art, that the debate "Is it art or isn't it?" went on for many decades, and photography was sort of pushed aside as something not quite up to snuff. I sometimes still think, "Is it an art or isn't it? Is it just artistic? What is the nature of art? What is the nature of survival?" But I don't dwell on this because it is not important. What is important is to preserve the images. At least they're there to look at and give some joy or insights to people.

When I was feeling down, I used to go upstairs to my studio and take out a handful of pictures—not just any pictures, I'd choose the ones I wanted to look at at that moment—and I would hold them in my hand and look at them, and suddenly a wave of comfort, a wave of reassurance, a wave of recognition would flow toward me, and I could say to myself, "I have made this. I did this." And like a miracle I felt comforted, reassured, useful, satisfied, uplifted, and that was enough. It was more than enough. I think I've had it all. I am filled with gratitude.

Photographs

A member of Youth Aliyah trains
in Germany for immigration to
Palestine, 1935

Dreaming of the Future

Wahn See, Berlin, 1933

The first German Youth Aliyah group in Palestine, Meshek Yagur, ca. 1933

Segregated Health Care

Jewish Hospital Infants' Nursery, Berlin, 1936

Segregated Education

A Jewish school class, Berlin, ca. 1936

opposite: *Segregated Sports*

Jews competing at the Grunewald
sports field, Berlin, ca. 1934

Maccabee sports field, Berlin, 1935

34

Youth Aliyah, ca. 1935

Martin Buber and students, Berlin, 1935

A man at a Jewish old age home in Berlin, 1934. This photograph was the first picture ever taken by Leni Sonnenfeld.

Painter Ludwig Meidner, Berlin, 1936

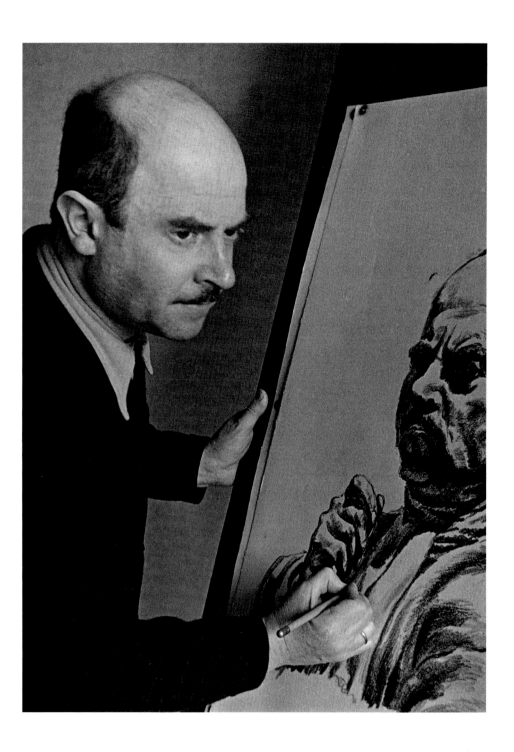

opposite: *Painter Max Lieberman, Brandenberger Tor, Berlin, 1934*

Members of Youth Aliyah embark for Palestine from Marseilles, ca. 1936

A boy at morning prayer on the Youth Aliyah train bound for Marseilles, ca. 1936

Berlin, ca. 1935

opposite: *Youth Aliyah teenagers
leave from Anhalter Bahnhof, Berlin,
ca. 1935, on a train bound for Marseilles,
the embarkation point for Palestine*

Waiting

Haifa Harbor, Palestine, 1938

Youth Aliyah members do their homework,
Kibbutz Degania, Palestine, 1937

opposite: *First scripture-reading lessons, Palestine, 1937*

Kibbutz Dalia, Palestine, ca. 1935

50

German refugees have their first Shabbat dinner
in America, New York, 1940

First impressions of New York,
winter 1940: fire escapes

Old Shoes for New

These individuals were among a group of nearly
a thousand refugees from Italian concentration
camps who arrived at Fort Ontario, near Oswego,
New York, ca. 1944

Many refugees were kept at Fort Ontario for nearly two years, during which time no visitors were permitted inside. Oswego, New York, ca. 1944.

A pioneer settlement from the founding days of the Zionist movement, Rosh Pina, Galilee, Israel, 1949

opposite: *Jerusalem marketplace, ca. 1934*

opposite: *Displaced Persons arrive in Palestine, ca. 1946*

*A yeshiva class studies the
Torah in Jerusalem, 1949*

opposite: *Veterans of the War of Independence,
Israel, 1948*

French refugees await embarkation, Marseilles, 1949

Marseilles, 1949

opposite: *Family members await incoming ships, Port of Haifa, Palestine, ca. 1946*

Port of Haifa, Palestine, ca. 1946

66

Port of Haifa, Israel, 1951

Port of Haifa, Israel, ca. 1951

opposite: *A Moroccan family arrives
in Port of Haifa, Israel, ca. 1949*

69

Port of Haifa, Israel, 1950s

70

opposite: *Camp Atlit, Israel, ca. 1951*

A Yemenite couple, Beersheba, Israel, 1949

opposite: *An emigrant from Iraq to Israel, ca. 1951*

opposite: *Workers hang their lunches in a
tree to deter insects in Galilee, Israel, 1953*

A fish farm near the Sea of Galilee,
Israel, ca. 1957

*Fishermen from Kibbutz Kishon at the Sea of
Galilee, Israel, ca. 1957*

opposite: *Galilee, near Safad, Israel, 1950s*

opposite: *Galilee, 1950s*

opposite: *Kibbutz Maagan Michael, Haifa, Israel, 1962*

Youth Aliyah training farm,
Cream Ridge, New Jersey, ca. 1953

88

An Israeli soldier on the troop train from Jerusalem to Haifa, 1965

opposite: *An Israeli soldier on desert maneuvers in the Negev, Israel, 1965*

Jerusalem, 1960s

Jerusalem, 1966

93

A bar mitzvah in Casablanca, Morocco, 1970

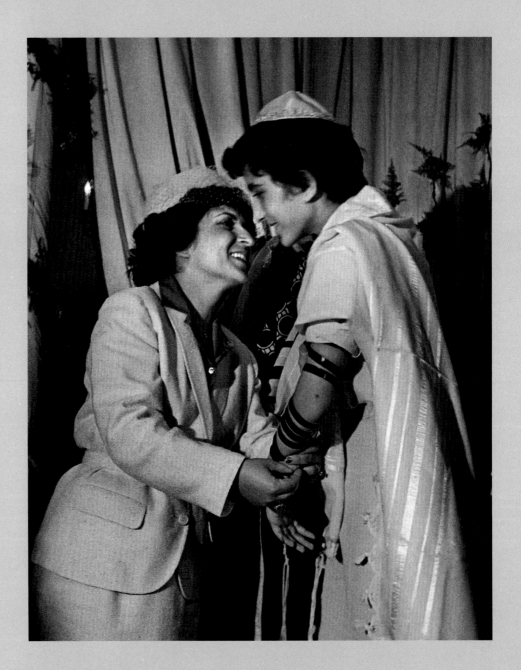

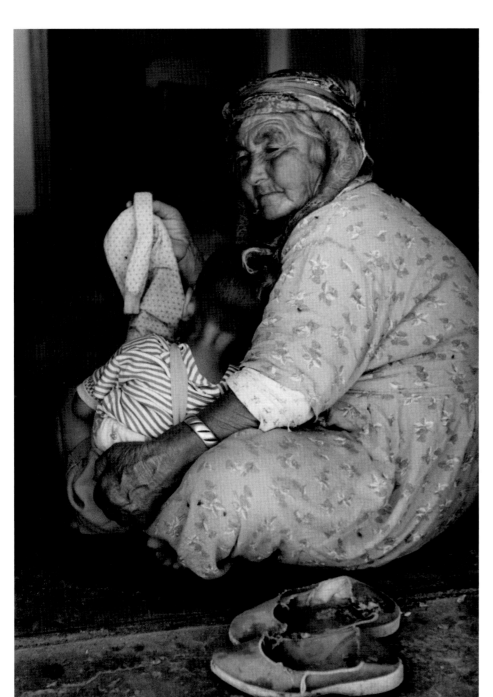

An Israeli grandmother in the Atlas Mountains, Morocco, ca. 1980

The Jewish Quarter, Tehran, Iran, 1980s

A Bedouin grandmother and little girl in the Negev Desert, Israel, 1972

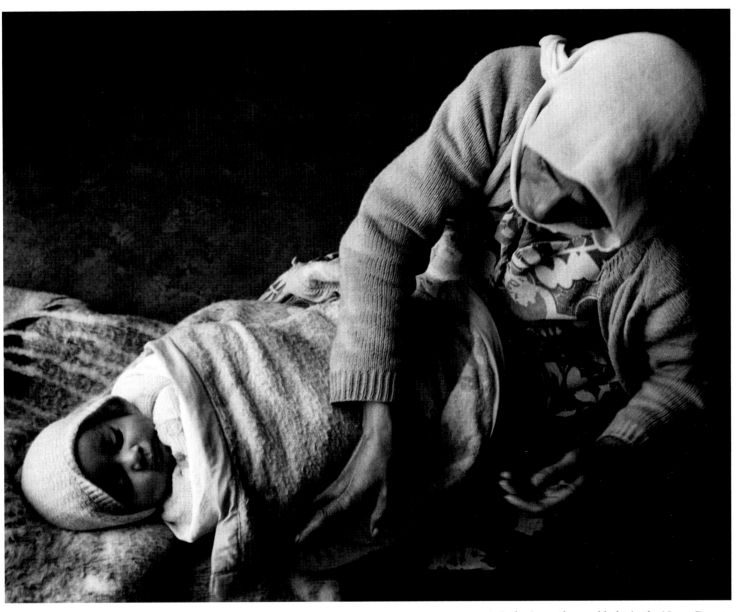

A Bedouin mother and baby in the Negev Desert, Israel, 1972

A Yemenite father and sons, Israel, 1964

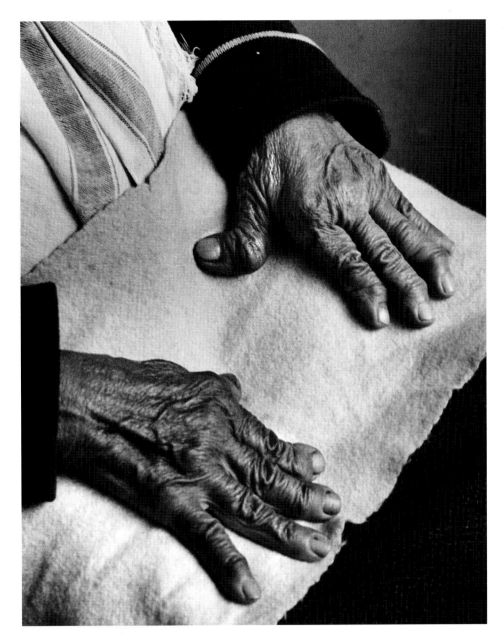

A Yemenite woman, Israel, 1970s

A road worker, Negev Desert, ca. 1972

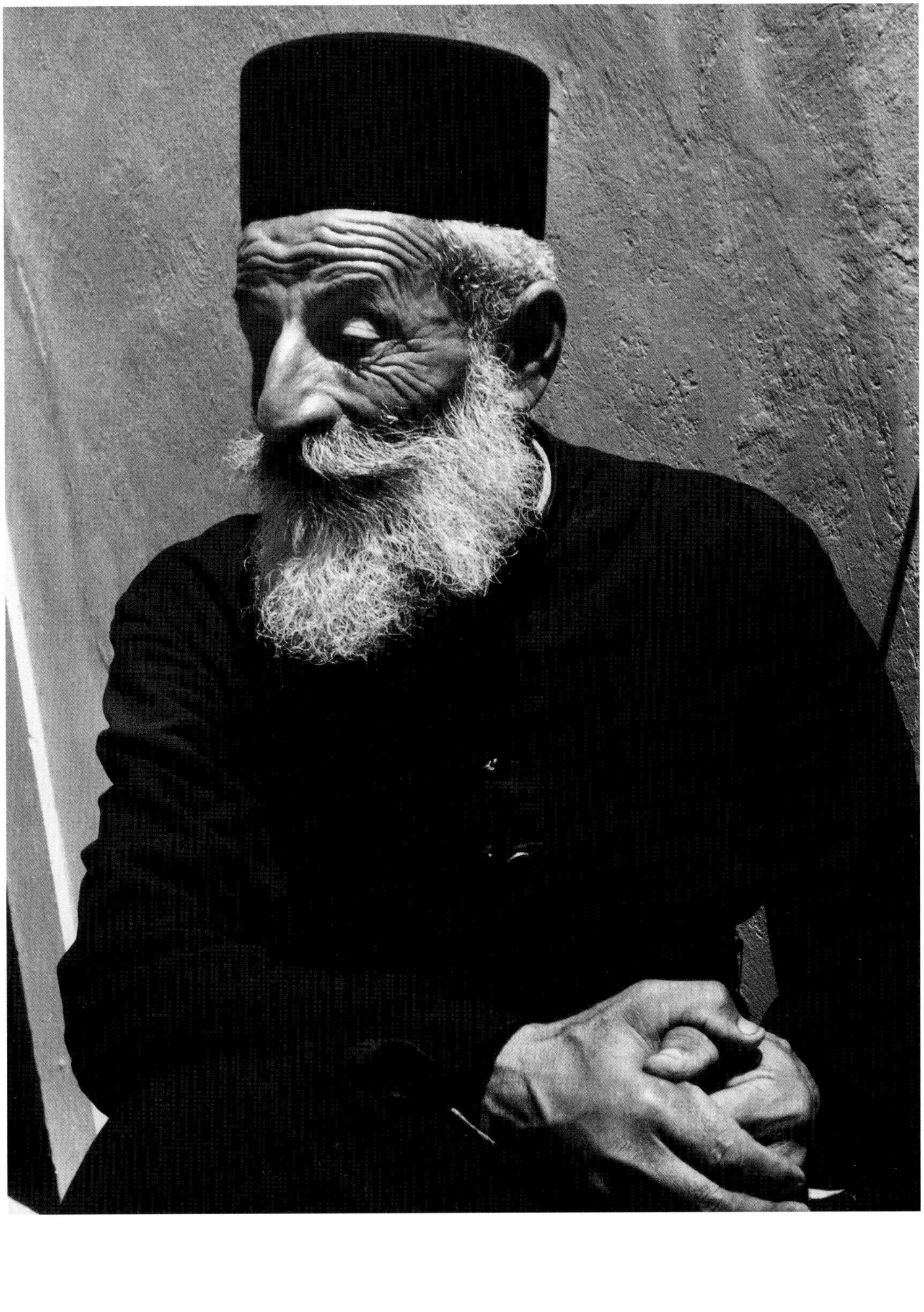

An Arab Maronite priest, Israel, 1970s

Arab marketplace, Hebron, West Bank,
Israel, 1980s

East Jerusalem marketplace, 1970s

opposite: *Israel, 1970s*

Two sisters make their home in an
abandoned building, Israel, 1940s

108

Fez, Morocco, 1973

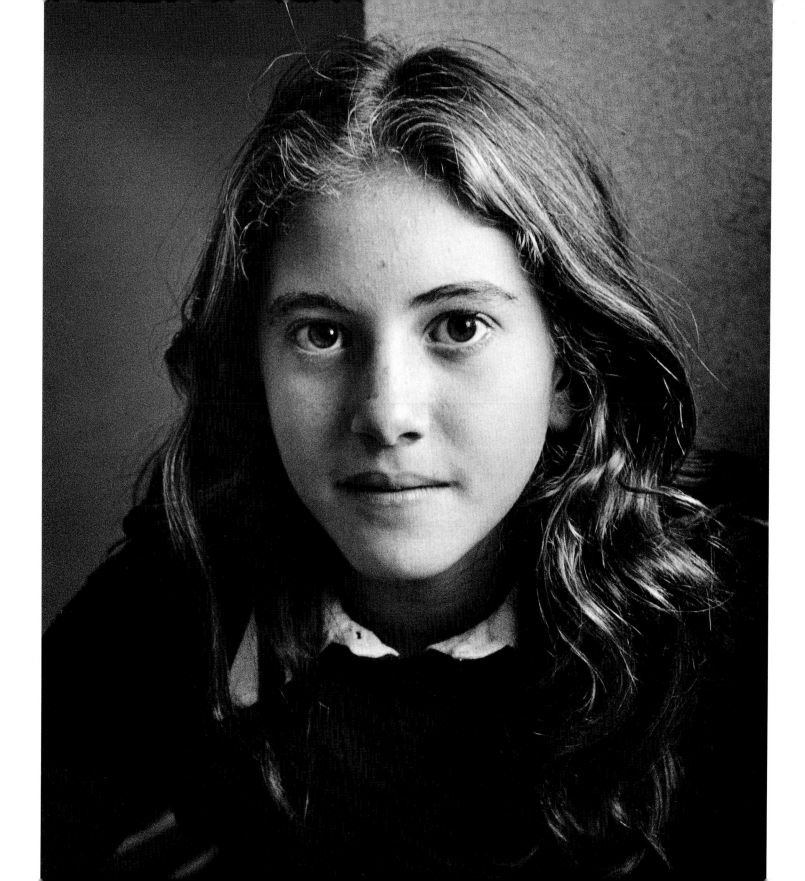

opposite: *A Jewish girl in Madrid, Spain, 1973*

Sardana dancers in Cathedral Square,
Barcelona, Spain, 1973

Cathedral Square, Barcelona, Spain, 1973

East Meets West

Israel, 1960s

116

New York City, 1972

Workers' Dance Hall, Marienbad,
Czechoslovakia, 1990

opposite: *The Wallflower*

Workers' Dance Hall, Marienbad,
Czechoslovakia, 1966

Ancient Watch Tree

Negev Desert, Israel, 1972

opposite: *Spain, along the road from Barcelona to Gerona, 1973*

Fez, Morocco, 1973

opposite: *The Jewish cemetery, Prague, ca. 1991*

The old Jewish ghetto, Gerona, Spain, 1973